941.83

DUNDRUM
THEN & NOW

HUGH ORAM

COLOUR PHOTOGRAPHY BY VINCENT CLARKE

The
History
Press
Ireland

First published 2015

The History Press Ireland
50 City Quay
Dublin 2
Ireland
www.thehistorypress.ie

© Hugh Oram, 2015
Colour photography © Vincent Clarke, 2015

The right of Hugh Oram to be identified as the Author
of this work has been asserted in accordance with the
Copyright, Designs and Patents Act 1988.

All rights reserved. No part of this book may be reprinted
or reproduced or utilised in any form or by any electronic,
mechanical or other means, now known or hereafter invented,
including photocopying and recording, or in any information
storage or retrieval system, without the permission in writing
from the Publishers.

British Library Cataloguing in Publication Data.
A catalogue record for this book is available from the British Library.

ISBN 978 1 84588 842 8

Typesetting and origination by The History Press

CONTENTS

ACKNOWLEDGEMENTS

FIRSTLY, I'D LIKE to thank my wife Bernadette for her patience and understanding while I was compiling and writing this book. As always, she has been an unerring guide along my journey. I'd like to give especial thanks to: James Burns, general manager, Milltown Golf Club; Tom Byrne, executive secretary of the Ten Pin Bowling Association; Peter Cassidy of the Dropping Well; Tony and Paddy Collins of Uncle Tom's Cabin; Tony Dempsey, of Roughan & O'Donovan, Sandyford, design engineers for the Dargan Luas bridge in Dundrum; Grants, Upper Baggot Street, Dublin 4, for all their help with the images (Grant Howie and Martin McElroy); Councillor Pat Hand, Dundrum; Kevin Harrington, Dundrum, author of *The Way to Dundrum*; Pat Herbert and Joe Guilfoyle, Ye Olde Hurdy Gurdy Wireless Museum, Howth; Shan Kelly, Windy Arbour Village Association; Catherine KilBride of Mount Anville; Pat Lafferty, Lafferty Associates, Dundrum; Ronan Lee, Dundrum; John G. Lennon, Dundrum & District Historical Society; Dean Lochner of the Bondi Group, Dublin 2, for his computing assistance; National Library of Ireland, especially Bernie Metcalfe; Ultan Mac Mathúna, principal, Holy Cross National School, Dundrum; Irene McGrane and Orla Hanratty at Airfield, as well as Grainne Millar, who used to run public relations at Airfield and now has her own consultancy; Christopher Moriarty, Churchtown Friends Meeting House (Quakers); Frank Mulvey of Mulvey's Pharmacy, Dundrum; Don Nugent, Jeanette Jordan (usually known simply as JJ) and Aideen Moran, all of Dundrum Town Centre; William O'Brien, senior assistant librarian in Dundrum Library; Peter Pearson, County Wexford, for permission to use photographs from his book, *Between the Mountains and the Sea*, first published in 1998; the staff of Pembroke Library, Anglesea Road, Dublin 4; Paddy Ryan of Ryan's Dundrum House and Ryan's Windy Arbour; and Chris Woods, headmaster, Wesley College, Ballinteer.

I'd like to thank the following who also helped considerably with the compilation of this book: Russell Bryce (Fianna Fáil headquarters) and Sara Scally, DMOD architects, Dublin, designers of Taney parish centre; Jen Cleary, Moss Cottage, Dundrum; Ciárán Cooney, honorary photographic archivist, Irish Railway Records Society, Dublin; Dave Downey (Dublin Book Browsers, Stillorgan); Dún Laoghaire-Rathdown County Council communications office; Pauline Kent, marketing officer, Dundrum Credit Union; John Lowe (moneydoctor.ie); Fr Donal McCarthy, Pallotine Fathers, Sandyford; Ken Mawhinney, An Taisce; Myra McPartlin, Mill Theatre, Dundrum Town Centre; Patricia Mellon, Broadway, County Wexford; Bronagh Moore (Irish Management Institute); Brenda O'Beirne, Holy Cross parish office, Dundrum; Oran O'Rua, Balally Players; and Roly Saul of the eponymous restaurant in Dundrum.

I am also indebted to *The Harcourt Street Line: Back on Track* (Currach Press, 2003) by Brian Mac Aongusa; *The Changing Face of Dundrum* (Elo Press, 1981) by Jim Nolan; *Dundrum* Boy (privately published, 2008) by John Mellon, and the Airfield Archives at NUI,Maynooth, for the old photographs of Airfield.

INTRODUCTION

ACCORDING TO LEGEND, Dundrum's history began in the seventh century AD, when St Nasi, sometimes called St Nahi, founded his monastery. It's long gone, but the church named after him is still a key historical place, close to the vast Luas bridge in Dundrum.

For centuries, right through the Middle Ages, life in Dundrum centred around Dundrum Castle, for long the home of the Fitzwilliam family. The ruins of the castle are still there, while another legacy of their estate are the various Pembroke estate cottages in Dundrum.

Big houses, with correspondingly big gardens, made up the largely rural area of Dundrum for many centuries and, even a century ago, the population of the village was still a mere 500. The large-scale housing developments that characterise Dundrum and surrounding neighbourhoods such as Balally and Ballinteer only started in the 1960s, bringing extensive population settlement in the Dundrum area.

Few of those big old houses still exist today; a rare exception to the widespread demolitions that took place is Airfield, once home to Letitia and Naomi Overend. Today, the fine house and its working farm have been meticulously restored by the Airfield Trust and new features added, such as the Overend Café.

The old-style village street in Dundrum has changed immeasurably and these days only one traditional-style shop remains: Campbell's Corner, the shoe repairer's, which has been on the site since 1900. When the Dundrum shopping centre was built in the early 1970s, it was a major changing point but, in turn, it was later dwarfed by the Dundrum Town Centre, which opened in March 2005. It's the largest shopping centre in Ireland and it has brought countless millions of shoppers to Dundrum; along with the shops, it houses approximately forty restaurants and a state-of-the-art theatre and cinema, which complement the much older facilities in Dundrum, such as the Carnegie Library, opened in 1914.

Today, the Dundrum Town Centre is by far the largest employer in the area, an accolade once held first by the Manor Mill Laundry, closed in 1942, and then by the Pye factory, itself closed over forty years later.

Just a few of the old-style buildings in Dundrum keep going, such as Ryan's pub on the Main Street and Uncle Tom's Cabin at Rosemount, just on the Dublin side of the Luas bridge. Dundrum also has a strong church heritage, with Holy Cross in Main Street and Christ Church at Taney, as well as much newer churches in such districts as Balally and Ballinteer.

These days, the Dundrum area is also renowned for its sporting links, including the Dundrum and South Dublin Athletic Club and Milltown Golf Club.

Dundrum remains an area that has seen tremendous development in the past half century, yet it still retains a unique sense of its antiquity, stretching back well over 1,000 years. Today, much in the Dundrum area is new, or relatively new, but many glimpses of the older, easy-going Dundrum with its country village way of life, can still be found.

THE OLD RAILWAY BRIDGE

THE RATHER SMALL railway bridge at the bottom of Dundrum's Main Street dated back to the opening of the old Harcourt Street railway line in 1854. The bridge spanned a narrow section of road at the junction of Dundrum Road and Taney Road. It was small, with room for just one line of traffic in each direction, but as the railway and road traffic was very infrequent in the years up to the 1950s it was sufficient.

In the late 1950s, the bridge was the scene of a tragic accident, when a CIE workman who was painting the underside of the bridge, fell and struck his head on the roadway. He was killed instantly.

The Harcourt Street line had its last rail traffic on 31 December 1958 and by the summer of 1960 the bridge had been demolished.

THE OLD RAILWAY bridge has now been replaced by the Luas bridge, which was completed in 2002, but which didn't come into use until 2004. After the closure of the old railway line, the embankments beside it were gradually chipped away, so that when it came to designing the new Luas bridge it had to span a 180-metre gap, making the new bridge over ten times longer than the old bridge. Today, a huge traffic junction lies beneath the bridge. The new junction is so vast that it's unwise for any pedestrian to attempt to cross it on foot. Another more recent feature is the small terminus area for buses close to the bridge, at the foot of Main Street.

LUAS BRIDGE BEING BUILT

DESIGN WORK ON the new Luas bridge at Dundrum began in 1996, although preliminary work on clearing the old trackbed of the Harcourt Street line did not begin until early 2000, with actual construction began the following year. The photograph shows the work underway close to Dundrum, on the Rosemount side of the village. Building the new track as far as the new station at Dundrum was relatively easy, but beyond the station it was much more difficult. The line goes through a deep cutting, which was cut into a spur of the Dublin mountains. Much rock removal work had to be done here in 2002 and 2003 to stabilise the sides of the cutting.

Roughan O'Donovan, based in Sandyford, designed the new cable-stay bridge. The first job was to build the 50-metre-tall concrete pylon, to which the stays of the bridge were attached. A total of forty-three concrete segments were fitted in place and connected to the cable stays to form the 180-metre span of the bridge. All these concrete segments, which were cast in Northern Ireland, were fitted in place at night, to avoid disrupting daytime road traffic beneath.

WORK ON THE bridge took eighteen months and was completed towards the end of 2002, but it wasn't until the Luas Green line was officially opened on 30 June 2004, that the bridge began to be used for regular tram services. Three weeks after the line was opened, the bridge was named after William Dargan, the great railway pioneer, who had lived in nearby Mount Anville house. The man who led the naming ceremony was the then Transport Minister, Seamus Brennan.

9

COLLISION ON THE OLD HARCOURT STREET LINE

THIS ACCIDENT HAPPENED on the evening of 23 December 1957, when one train ran into the back of another in the cutting beyond Dundrum station. A cow had been spotted wandering on the line, so a train approaching from Bray was travelling very slowly. The rear oil lamp on this train should have been replenished at Bray, but wasn't, so the driver of a second train, also coming from Bray, but much faster, failed to see the first train in time. The driver of this second train, Andy Larkin, was killed and the guard on the first train as well as three passengers were injured but not seriously. However, the damage to the trains was severe and the tracks were so badly damaged that full services didn't resume until after Christmas.

THE 1957 COLLISION just beyond Dundrum station on the old railway line caused one of the rare fatalities on the old Harcourt Street line. That enviable safety record has been replicated

on the Green Luas line, which is operated by the Transdev company. Trams on this 16.5-kilometre-long line travel the best part of 2 million km a year, between Bride's Glen and St Stephen's Green. Work on connecting the Green and Red Luas lines in Dublin city centre is well advanced. But the Green Luas line has fourteen signalled road junctions, compared with forty-eight on the Red line, so there's much less chance of a collision with a car or other vehicle. It's also estimated that the chance of a person and a tram making contact on the Green Line is about once in every 1 million kilometres. So the accident rate on the Green Line is far lower than on the Red Line.

ST NASI'S CHURCH

THE ORIGINAL ST NASI'S (sometimes called St Nahi's) church and its adjoining monastery were the two earliest buildings in Dundrum, dating from about AD 600, or about 1,400 years ago. All trace of them has long since vanished. The present church, with its simple boxlike structure, dates from the early eighteenth century; the earliest grave there is dated 1734. Among the church's artefacts is the font in which the Duke of Wellington was baptised in 1769; it came from an old church in Camden Row in the city centre.

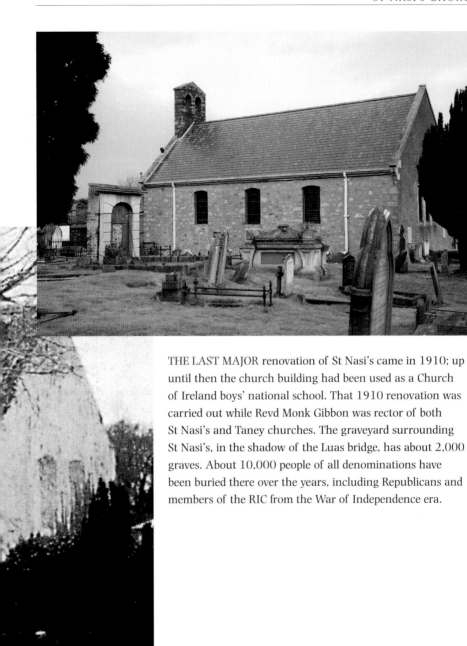

THE LAST MAJOR renovation of St Nasi's came in 1910; up until then the church building had been used as a Church of Ireland boys' national school. That 1910 renovation was carried out while Revd Monk Gibbon was rector of both St Nasi's and Taney churches. The graveyard surrounding St Nasi's, in the shadow of the Luas bridge, has about 2,000 graves. About 10,000 people of all denominations have been buried there over the years, including Republicans and members of the RIC from the War of Independence era.

DUNDRUM'S MAIN STREET

MAIN STREET IN Dundrum is a mishmash of architectural styles, from the modern brick of the college of further education to the Dundrum Village Centre, the old shopping centre left stranded by the creation of the Dundrum Town Centre. The Town Centre end of the Main Street has a number of distinctive architectural features, including the Pembroke Cottages, the Catholic church and Ryan's pub, that go back to Victorian times, but more modern buildings have made little effort to blend in with this architectural heritage.

SOME OF THE earlier terraces of houses still exist on Main Street today, but they are overshadowed by more modern buildings. The only traditional shop left on the street is Campbell's Corner, the shoe repair shop at the crossroads. The street also has other well-known outlets, such as Burdock's fish and chip shop, close to Campbell's, as well as the charity shops Women's Aid, Christian Aid, Dundrum Village charity shop, Human Appeal (in the nearby Apollo Building) and Oxfam. But the overall impression of Main Street is that it is devoid of any sense of visual unity in its mélange of architectural styles, old and new. When the Dundrum Town Centre was being planned, upgrades were promised to the street furniture and general appearance of Main Street, but these were delayed by the subsequent recession.

DUNDRUM'S OLD RAILWAY STATION

WHEN THE OLD railway line from Harcourt Street opened in 1854, Dundrum was meant to be the end of the line, so on the Taney side of that line, an impressive single-storey station was built. It had better facilities than any other station on the line, which ended up serving Bray. It so happened that William Dargan, the builder of the line, lived at nearby Mount Anville and used the station regularly to get to and from town, another factor in ensuring that the station had excellent facilities.

Long before the line closed at the end of 1958, the station had sprouted many large enamel advertising signs, as well as a sign proclaiming that this was the station for St Columba's College, about 5km distant. The station platform also had a variety of machines that told fortunes, embossed names on metal tape and dispensed chocolate, coffee and chewing gum.

AFTER THE CLOSURE of the old railway line, the main station building was put to a variety of uses, including as the headquarters of Carr Communications, a public relations firm founded by Bunny Carr. He had previously been the compere of the *Quicksilver* quiz show on Irish television, from where originated the much-used phrase of the time, 'Stop the lights'.

With the building of the Luas, the old building on the Taney Road side of the line was retained and today houses a café, while the building on the other side of the line was demolished and replaced by a small shelter.

DUNDRUM CREDIT UNION

THIS HOUSE WAS built in the mid-nineteenth century as the family home of William Richardson, who also used it as the base for his very successful building business. The exact date the house was built has never been discovered. It was reputed to have been the first house in Dundrum to have been built with a slate roof. Many of the redbrick houses built in and around Dundrum in the late nineteenth and early twentieth centuries were the work of the Richardsons. Eventually, William Richardson's son, John Paul, took over the running of the business; he and his wife Ellen Mary had eleven children and the boys were the next generation to take over when John Paul died in 1930. When the last of the Richdardsons to have lived in the house died in 1980, it was sold to the Dundrum Credit Union.

THE DUNDRUM CREDIT Union
began, in 1966, like various other
'institutions' in Dundrum, in the
Carnegie Library, with the sum
of £1 on deposit. After the credit
union moved into the Richardsons'
old house in 1986, the premises
became its first office proper.
The house was extended, but the
poor structural quality of the
original building encouraged the
credit union to knock it down and
rebuild on the same site. The credit
union now extends to Ballinteer,
Rathfarnham and Knocklyon, as well
as to UCD's Belfield campus, and its
assets are reportedly worth over
€80 million. The general Dundrum
area has a second credit union,
covering Milltown and Clonskeagh,
with an office at Milltown.

SINGAPORE GARDENS CHINESE RESTAURANT

WHAT HAD BEEN Cooper's restaurant and café at 15 Main Street was turned into the Singapore Gardens in 1992. Paul Campbell remembers it as a luxurious, well-appointed restaurant that created a real stir as the first restaurant of its kind in Dundrum. It was

also used for several years as the launching place for the Dundrum Festival. However, despite being in a new building that replaced the house that had stood on the site, its tenure was short, just five years.

BY 1999, IT had been transformed into the Emerald Gardens Chinese restaurant. The site was subsequently redeveloped and now houses the Sports Nutrition store and the Cedars Beauty Clinic.

CAMPBELL'S CORNER

CAMPBELL'S CORNER, A shoe repair shop, has been at the crossroads on Dundrum's
Main Street for over 100 years and is the last traditional business remaining in
Main Street. But the business is far older than that; by 1849, it was already established in
the Parliament Street area of the city centre. The grandfather of the man who now runs
the shop, Paul Campbell, was Patrick Campbell and in 1900, he decided to move the shop,
which then made shoes for men and women, to Dundrum, because the much purer air
there suited his bronchial condition far better. When the Dundrum shop opened, it was
in the name of Patrick's brother Michael, because Patrick had also become the master
shoemaker at the asylum in Windy Arbour.

This photograph, taken in 1908, shows Paul Campbell's father Jack (second from right). Paul has been involved in the shop all his life and he says that until quite recently, the shop had gas, but no electricity.

PAUL AND HIS wife Florrie are still in residence, but their son, also Paul, who worked in the Dundrum shop for twenty-six years, now has his own shoe and shoe-repair business in Enniscorthy, County Wexford. Paul senior is one of the well-known characters in Dundrum and he was also Mayor of Dundrum for two years running in 2009 and 2010.

OLD COTTAGES BY DUNDRUM TOWN CENTRE

THESE COTTAGES ARE identical in style to the Pembroke Cottages on nearby
Main Street and were built at the same time. Two of the cottages front onto the start
of Ballinteer Road, beside an entrance to the Dundrum Town Centre and close to the
bridge over the Dundrum bypass. These cottages were built in the 1870s and '80s for

the Pembroke estate which, at the time, was the largest family owned estate in south County Dublin. They were built for workers and labourers on the estate, but the rents were high for the time, nearly three shillings a week. The cottages were solidly built from stone and the bricks used were supplied by the local and now long-defunct bricksworks. The roofs were slated, an innovation at the time. The cottages were all built by John Richardson, whose building firm and family home were on the Main Street, where the credit union now stands. The architect of the cottages is unknown, but the construction work was supervised by James Owen, an architect with the then Board of Works, now the Office of Public Works. After they had been completed, he said that the work had been well done and he commended the cottages for being light and airy.

TODAY, BOTH OF the cottages are occupied by the Mud Pie beauty boutique. Behind them are four more identical cottages, which today house the Port House Ibéricos restaurant, which serves wines and tapas.

DUNDRUM'S CARNEGIE LIBRARY

THE CARNEGIE LIBRARY in Dundrum was one of sixty-eight such libraries built throughout Ireland during the first two decades of the twentieth century, thanks to the generosity of Andrew Carnegie, a Scottish-American philanthropist who became one of the richest men in America, through his investments in railroads, steel making and other enterprises.

Rudolf Maximilian Butler (1872–1943), Dublin architect and Professor of Architecture at what is now UCD, designed the library building to have Doric columns flanking its main entrance and above that entrance, an oval window with ornamental plasterwork.

The opening of the library was conducted by the Lord Chancellor on 12 August 1914, less than a fortnight after the start of the First World War. The upper floor of the library had a stage and in the 1920s and 1930s, the library was the main entertainment centre in Dundrum, before the opening of the Odeon cinema. Local drama groups often put on plays and pantomimes at Christmas, while concerts were organised by Cathal McGarvey. Irish step dancing classes were also organised by a local man, 'Jem' Byrne, and the library was also home to the Dundrum Ceili Band. In the 1920s, the library was also used for vocational education classes, which led to the local vocational school being set up.

BY THE LATE 1960s, the glory days of the library were long past and the place was closed for several years. It was completely renovated in 1973 and since its reopening has once again become a hub for the local community. These days, it's much more than a place to borrow books; it has a substantial local history section, maps and computers. Many local groups use the library, including parents and toddlers, Scrabble devotees, Irish language conversationalists, budding writers and a book club.

MILL HOUSE

MILL HOUSE, ON the Sandyford Road, just past the crossroads in Dundrum, dates back to at least 1736, probably earlier, and is the oldest building in the vicinity of Dundrum's Main Street, apart from Dundrum Castle. Its name indicates that it was connected with the mills that once stood nearby in the eighteenth and early nineteenth centuries, and it probably housed the miller and his family.

An 1837 survey said that the Mill House was only one of four houses in this part of Dundrum with a slate roof. The house was also known for its large fruit and vegetable garden; the gardener lived in a gate lodge beside the back gate to the garden. The area of

the garden is now occupied by the Mill Pond in the Dundrum Town Centre.

After the establishment of the Manor Mill Laundry in 1864, Mill House was used by the Edmondson family, who owned and ran the laundry, and the terrace outside was used for washing and drying linen. During the later twentieth century, the house was owned and occupied by the Dillon family; Dr Dillon Digby, who had been a managing director of the Pye factory nearby, was in residence there through the 1990s.

TODAY, THE FAÇADE of the building is a protected structure. The building is occupied by Roly Saul's restaurant and has been extensively developed with a conservatory-style extension at the back.

29

MILLTOWN VIADUCT

THE MILLTOWN VIADUCT dates back over 150 years; it was built
for the Harcourt Street to Dundrum railway line, opened in 1854.
After that railway closed, at the end of 1958, the old railway bridge
at Dundrum was demolished in the summer of 1960, but the stone
structure of the viaduct at Milltown was so extensive that it was left
intact, making it the only major piece of infrastructure that survived.
It had also survived the Second World War; holes had been drilled in
the base of the viaduct, which, in the event of a UK or German invasion
of Ireland, would have been filled with explosives to blow up the bridge.
Those holes can still be seen today.

THE VIADUCT GOT a new lease of life when the Luas Green line opened
in 2004. When it was reopened for Luas use, it had only needed a small
amount of refurbishment; the main structure was still in excellent
condition, after more than 100 years. Beside the present-day viaduct
is the large chimney that is the only surviving relic of the old Milltown
Laundry. Extensive apartment development now covers the site.

DROPPING WELL

THE DROPPING WELL pub at Milltown dates back to 1847; its first use was as a morgue
for the bodies of famine victims being washed down the River Dodder. The bodies were
wrapped in winding sheets before being buried in a nearby mass grave. After the famine,
it became a pub and the name was changed to the Dropping Well in 1907. Early in
the twentieth century, the pub was owned by a man called Meagher who was a noted
boxer; he had a boxing ring built in the pub so customers could challenge him to a fight.
The owner inevitably won. A section of the pub, Boxer Maher's, is named after him and is
given over to many old photos and other artefacts.

TODAY THE PUB is owned by Charlie Chawke, a native of Adare, County Limerick, and it's one of close on a dozen pubs he owns in the Dublin area. He is regarded as one of the most innovative publicans in a trade that has been badly hit by the recessionary downturn. The Dropping Well has preserved its nineteenth-century atmosphere and design, while the facilities have been much upgraded to include a number of dining rooms and function areas. The pub serves food, all day, every day as well as putting on many musical events, and it is always busy with weddings and other functions. Just at the back of the pub, languishing in the waters of the River Dodder, is a statue of a rhino; no one is quite sure how it got there.

CLASSON'S BRIDGE

CLASSON'S BRIDGE DATES back to the eighteenth century and is named after the man who owned the nearby brickworks. The original bridge was destroyed in 1921, during the War of Independence. Many unsuccessful attempts had been made to blow up the bridge, before the span finally collapsed into the River Dodder. It took until 1928 to repair the bridge, and a plaque on the bridge notes this date. Until it was repaired, people had to tread on planks laid across the gap, making access to Milltown golf course from the Milltown direction very difficult. Ballinteer and Rathfarnham have similar old-style bridges.

CLASSON'S BRIDGE HAD a considerable renovation in the summer of 2014, although this was confined mainly to footpath upgrading. The structure of the bridge remains essentially as it was following the 1928 reconstruction. When the bridge was rebuilt, no one could have foreseen that nearly ninety years later, it would be totally inadequate for the volumes of traffic travelling to and from Churchtown. The bridge remains barely wide enough to take two opposing lanes of traffic. The view from the bridge looking upstream, on the same side as the adjacent Dropping Well pub, is much hindered by rampant foliage growing along the riverbanks, but the 'rhino in the river' can be clearly seen.

MOUNT ANVILLE

THE ORIGINAL HOUSE at Mount
Anville dates back to the last decade of
the eighteenth century. It had various
occupiers before William Dargan,
the railway pioneer. One early owner
of Mount Anville was Henry Roe,
a wealthy Dublin whiskey distiller, who
employed a French chef called Michel
Jammet; he went on to found the
noted Dublin restaurant of that name.
William Dargan and his wife Jane
entertained Queen Victoria at Mount
Anville in 1853, but he refused the offer
of a baronetcy that the queen made to
him there.

On 1 May 1865, while Dargan
was riding on the Stillorgan Road,
a housemaid opened the bedroom
window of a house to shake out the bed
sheets. This frightened his horse, which
threw Dargan to the ground, badly

injuring him. He never recovered and soon afterwards sold Mount Anville to the Society of the Sacred Heart.

IN THE YEARS since, Mount Anville has become one of the most prestigious fee-paying girls' secondary schools in Dublin. In 2007, the society handed over the running of the school to a trust, which maintains its educational ethos. Among the alumni of the school are Catherine Day, Secretary-General of the European Commission, and Mary Robinson, a former President of Ireland.

IRISH MANAGEMENT INSTITUTE

THIS RENOWNED SEAT of learning for people working at management level was founded
in 1952 and, for twenty years, moved between various city centre buildings. Before it
moved to Sandyford, its last place of residence had been what is now the Russian Embassy
on Orwell Road. Its brand new premises at Sandyford was constructed in the grounds of
Clonard, a fine Victorian mansion, which stands to this day, one of the few big houses in
the Dundrum area to survive intact from Victorian times. The buildings were designed

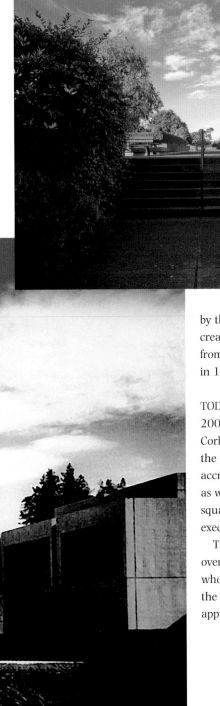

by the Arthur Gibney architectural practice, which created a very modern-looking building, constructed from concrete. The new premises was opened in 1974.

TODAY, THE INSTITUTE is still going strong. In 2009, it formed a link with University College, Cork, formalised into an alliance in 2011. Today, the majority of degrees awarded by the Institute are accredited by the Cork university. The centre itself, as well as its conference facilities, cover 53,000 square metres and includes fifty bedrooms for executives attending its courses.

The Institute has produced many fine characters over the years, including the late Diarmuid O'Broin, who for many years ran the commercial side of the institute's own magazine, which was called, appropriately enough, *Management*.

CLONARD HOUSE

WHEN THE IRISH Management Institute decided to relocate to Sandyford, it bought a large mansion called Clonard and its estate. The old house dates back to Victorian times and was once the home of Henry Thompson, a noted wine merchant in Dublin, whose firm, Thompson and D'Olier, was once one of the best known in Dublin. When the institute had its new headquarters built almost beside Clonard, it retained the old house for use as offices.

THE HOUSE IS still there today, a rare example of one of Dundrum's old big houses surviving into the twenty-first century. Further down the Sandyford Road, another big house, Moreen, which dated from the late eighteenth century, didn't survive. Instead, its estate is now occupied by the currency production unit of the Central Bank of Ireland.

AIRFIELD

AIRFIELD HOUSE AND estate today form a unique heritage site, where visitors can get an insight into life in old-time Dundrum. A wealthy Dublin solicitor, Trevor Overend, bought the old farmhouse in 1894 and had it converted into a fine, commodious house. The land surrounding the house covered a mere 3 ha, but it was subsequently extended to 15 ha. Trevor Overend's two daughters, Letitia and Naomi, lived in the house for the rest of their lives; Letitia died in 1977, Naomi in 1993. Long before they died, they had drawn up plans for the house and estate to be taken over after their deaths by the Airfield Trust, which still runs them today.

THE HOUSE ITSELF has been sympathetically restored, with all its old furniture and fittings in place. The sisters never threw out anything of interest, so all kinds of memorabilia, like old newspaper copies, can be seen today. Touchscreen interactive technology makes it very easy for visitors of all ages to delve into the history of the house and estate, and they can then relax and enjoy produce from the farm at the new Overend Café close by.

AIRFIELD AND
THE OVERENDS

THE TWO OVEREND sisters had a gilded life, far removed from that of ordinary working people in the Dundrum area. They never needed to work, so were able to indulge their interest in travel. But they also did much charitable work; during the First World War, the sisters looked after the many soldiers sent to the house to recover from their battle injuries. Letitia was also very involved with the St John's Ambulance Brigade. In 1920, she was offered an OBE for all her charity work, but she declined.

The sisters had a great passion for cars and possessed three splendid examples from the 1920s. When Naomi came back from a tour of India in 1936, she was given a present of an Austin 10 Tickford, which she drove for the rest of her life. The sisters also owned a Peugeot 172 Quadrellete Baby Quad, nicknamed the 'Flea', which had been bought new in 1923 for £230. The biggest car of the three was the Rolls-Royce 209, bought in London in 1927. This was driven by Letitia for the rest of her life and even today, people in Dundrum have stories about how she used to drive it down to the Main Street in Dundrum and park it there in a haphazard way. That was long before there was much traffic in Dundrum and well before traffic wardens had been thought of.

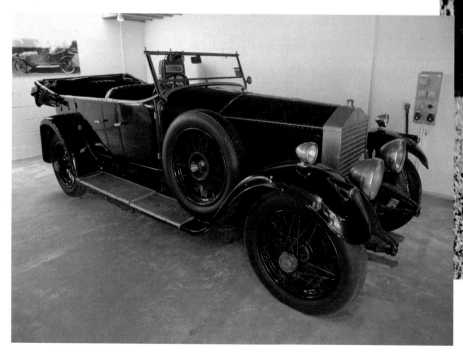

THE THREE CARS are still in excellent mechanical condition and are on display in the new garage at Airfield, which also uses touchscreen interactive technology to tell the fascinating story of those cars.

MELLON'S OLD GARAGE

MELLON'S SERVICE GARAGE was in Main Street, close to the crossroads, and on the same side as Campbell's Corner. It was started by John Mellon, who came to Dundrum in the late 1890s; by 1900, he was living at No. 1 Ashgrove Terrace. He started in business hiring out horse-drawn carriages, with some of those cabs based at railway stations, including that in Dundrum. When cars came in, he bought two. In time, the business developed further, expanding into selling petrol and doing repairs. By the late 1930s, Mellon's was still one of the few garage businesses in south County Dublin.

During the Emergency period of the Second World War, when petrol wasn't available except for some professionals like GPs and district nurses, the business managed to survive, with various members of the Mellon family in charge, led by Paddy Mellon. As a diversification, a sawmill was established at the back of the garage; since coal was in short supply, there was a roaring trade for its logs.

THE GARAGE CAME to a dramatic end in 1956. After Paddy Mellon died, his widow claimed that the business belonged to her. The rest of the family argued that since John Mellon, the founder, had died intestate, all members of the family should inherit it. The case came to court and was decided in favour of Paddy Mellon's widow. However, none of the old customers supported her; the boycott of the business was complete and it collapsed, amid bitterness that lasted for years. John Mellon, pictured here, the grandson of the founder of Mellon's Garage, died in 2010.

GALLAGHER'S OLD SHOP

GALLAGHER'S OLD SHOP,
which sold groceries
and stationery, stood on
Main Street in Dundrum,
where the AIB branch is
now located. At one time,
it was also the location for
the post office. In the old
photograph, members of
the Royal Irish Constabulary
from Dundrum barracks on
the Upper Kilmacud Road are
seen outside the shop. When
Gallagher's was thriving,
in the early twentieth century,
another popular shop was
Walsh's fish shop, which
had a good trade for years,
especially on Fridays. Also
close to Gallagher's was a

chemist's shop, run by a Miss Jones. Continuing down the Main Street at this point was a much more eccentric shop, that of Davy Dillon. He stocked a meagre amount of groceries and kept the shop open for conversational rather than trading reasons. Davy liked to talk with his customers but if they came in while he was reading a piece in a newspaper, he'd tell them to wait until he was finished! His eccentricity was marked in other ways, too; he wore an old-fashioned wing collar and kept the two parts of the collar fastened with a pin. Also near Gallagher's shop was Conaty's butchers, a noted retail fixture in old Dundrum.

THE FACE OF retailing in this of retailing in this part of the Main Street has changed utterly during the past three decades. Today a branch of AIB bank is the main feature, situated next to the K-Nails beauty salon and the Namasté Indian restaurant. Next comes a branch of the EBS building society (now part of AIB), the Dublin Alterations Centre and Callaghans (robemakers), followed by a very modern outfit, the Dundrum Tattoo Studio. McCanns Cleaners and Mannions solicitors.

MANOR MILL LAUNDRY

THE MANOR MILL Laundry, close to where the pond is situated in the present-day Dundrum Town Centre, was started in 1864 by the Edmundson family, who were also closely involved with the old laundry at Milltown. The Manor Mill Laundry turned out to be a thriving concern and managed to survive for nearly eight decades, until it finally closed because of wartime shortages in 1942. But for many years before that, it was the largest employer in the Dundrum area, having, at its peak, about 400 employees, mostly women, on its payroll.

The Manor Mill Laundry served not only a large part of south County Dublin, but covered much of County Wicklow. Customers could have their laundry collected from homes or businesses by the laundry's fleet of horse-drawn carts, or if they were

convenient to the railway, use that method for sending their washing to the laundry. Each item was carefully tagged, so that it could be returned to customers in pristine condition.

ALMOST AS SOON as the laundry closed down, its premises were taken over for the Pye factory, which in turn also became Dundrum's largest employer, employing 1,200 at its high point. The chimney stack of the old Milltown Laundry can still be seen beside the Luas viaduct over the River Dodder. Today it is the site of Dundrum Town Centre, Ireland's largest shopping complex. It has numerous well-known international and Irish retailing brand names and close on 20 million people visit every year. Many visitors arrive by car, from all over the greater Dublin area (indeed all different parts of Ireland), and the centre has 3,400 car parking spaces.

MANOR MILL
LAUNDRY WASHROOM

THE WASHROOM IN the laundry was the worst part of the building for workers; as its name implied, this is where the laundry was washed, a largely manual process for many years. Until the Manor Mill Laundry closed in 1942, it provided much life for the nearby Main Street. With some 500 people on its payroll, when lunchtime many of those workers made their way to Main Street, chatting away, perhaps having a smoke, or popping into one of the then numerous small shops. After the laundry came the Pye works, but that tradition of lunchtime browsing was less obvious. After the Pye works closed down, some of that factory space was turned into the Dundrum Bowl, but its longevity was short lived, abbreviated by the frequent floods from the River Slang. After the bowling alley came Super Crazy Prices, one of the first discount supermarkets in Ireland. But for long years subsequently, the site remained undeveloped, the subject of a protracted planning tribunal.

IN 1999, BUILDING work on Dundrum Town Centre started. The main complex opened on 3 March 2005, with other facilities such as the cinema and theatre following shortly afterwards. Today, the centre is by far the largest employer in the area; between its shops, its leisure facilities and various commercial organisations it now employs close on 6,000 people.

CHURCH OF IRELAND PRIMARY SCHOOL AT TANEY

TANEY'S CHURCH OF Ireland primary school goes back to 1792, if not earlier. It became a national school in 1898. Six years after the new church was built in Taney in 1818, a sexton's cottage was built beside it. For many years, the sexton's house was used as an infants' school. As for the main primary school, it was in a fine Gothic style schoolhouse at Eglinton Terrace from 1897 and remained there until pressure of numbers necessitated a brand new school at Sydenham Villas, opened in 1970. Substantial expansion took place during the 1990s and subsequently.

The photographs show the old sexton's cottage, now a domestic residence, beside the church at Taney, as well as the class of 1947 in Taney national school.

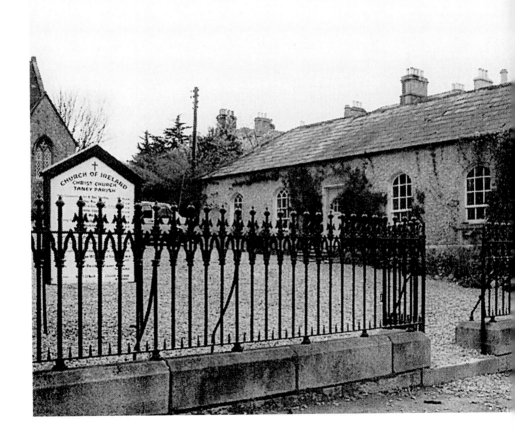

TODAY'S CHURCH OF Ireland Taney parish school at Sydenham Villas bears little if any resemblance to the original school here, founded as a parochial and charitable school for the underprivileged. The present-day school, whose principal is Mrs Elizabeth Carter, is a co-educational primary school in the State education system. It has around 450 pupils and just over twenty teachers, with eight grades running from junior infants to sixth classes. The school's patron remains the Church of Ireland Archbishop of Dublin and Glendalough. The present buildings at Sydenham Villas were opened in 1970, as a six-teacher school; they were subsequently extended in 1994.

THE USHER MONUMENT

THIS MONUMENT, AT the foot of Main Street, Dundrum, commemorates a local doctor who was killed in 1917. Dr Isaac Usher was a popular GP in the area, who was notorious for being late. One day, he was rushing to catch a train when he was knocked down by a car; he was one of the first motoring fatalities in Ireland. This northern end of Main Street once had one of Dundrum's two crossroads, and a monument in his honour was placed in the middle of the crossroads. It had a water trough so that horses could quench their thirst, and drinking cups so that humans could do likewise.

THE MONUMENT WAS subsequently moved and now stands outside the Ulster Bank branch in Usher House, just at the entrance to the Luas station, but it no longer has fresh flowing water.

DROMMARTIN CASTLE

THE NAME OF Drommartin has been connected with the Dundrum area since the
eighteenth century. In 1781, Lord Fitzwilliam granted Patrick D'Arcy permission to
construct a brickworks at Drommartin and the castle was built at around the same time,
probably by D'Arcy the brickmaker. It had an unusual façade, with very wide windows.
The adjoining Birch's Lane, between Taney Road and Upper Kilmacud Road, is called after
Henry Birch, who lived in the castle in the 1860s. The house, on the east side of Birch's
Lane, was demolished in 1984.

IN PLACE OF the long demolished Drommartin Castle, several housing schemes have been built and a number of new roads opened up, including Birchfield Avenue, Court, Heights, Lane and Park, which are on the opposite side of Birch's Lane to the old castle. A small complex of houses and apartments has been built almost on the site of the old castle, retaining an almost identical name, Dromartin Castle, while the cul-de-sac on this side of the lane is called Silver Birches. Some commercial companies, too, have based themselves in this immediate area, which is only about two minutes' walk from the Luas station at Dundrum.

Any comparison between Birch's Lane in the old days, with the occasional big house like Drommartin Castle, and few other buildings, and today's heavily developed area, is impossible. For many decades, the lane beside the old castle, connecting Taney Road and the Upper Kilmacud Road, was called Birch's Lane; it is still called that on Ordnance Survey maps. But the modern spelling of the name is usually 'Birches'.

WYCKHAM

THIS FINE THREE-STOREYED house was built about 1800 and much enlarged during the nineteenth century. It stands on Ballinteer Road, close to the Dundrum bypass. The house had various owners during the nineteenth century, including Sir Edward Kinahan, who bought it in 1873; he had a thriving wine and spirit business at the corner of D'Olier Street and Burgh Quay. That site is now occupied by O'Connell Bridge House.

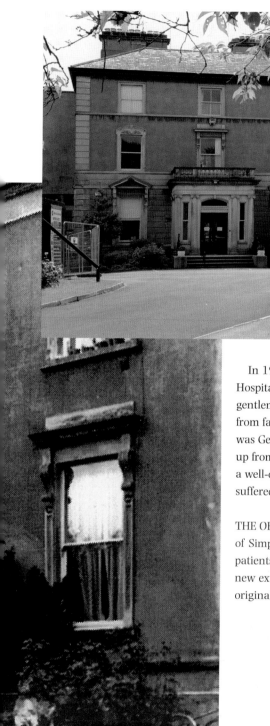

In 1925, the house was bought by Simpson's Hospital, which had been founded in 1791 for gentlemen of reduced circumstance suffering from failing eyesight, gout or both. Its benefactor was George Simpson, who had worked his way up from being a penniless, homeless orphan to a well-off draper and philanthropist, and who suffered from these two medical conditions.

THE ORIGINAL HOUSE still stands at the heart of Simpson's Hospital, which now caters for patients of both sexes. In recent years, significant new extensions have been built alongside the original house.

LUDFORD, NOW WESLEY COLLEGE

THIS FINE OLD house was built in 1815 as the farmhouse for Ludford Farm in Ballinteer. Wesley College was founded in 1845, and for many years was based at St Stephen's Green. By the 1920s, it had started expanding into the Upper Leeson Street area, where the college had extensive operations. One of its sites there was where the Burlington Hotel was subsequently built in 1972. In 1964, the college had decided to move out of town to the Dundrum area and that year paid the grand sum of £55,000 for the 20 hectares of Ludform Farm for its new educational complex. Ludford House was turned into the

headmaster's residence and the first headmaster to live there was the Revd Gerald G. Myles. After him, four further headmasters were in residence there, including Kenneth G. Blackmore (1977-1996) and Dr John W. Harris (1996-2003).

THE PRESENT HEADMASTER, Chris Woods, took up the position in 2003 and ever since then, the house has been the residence of the Woods family. The house itself is a protected structure. Although a new roof and new windows have been added in the past decade, its basic structure has changed little over the years. However, from the outside, the house looks bigger than it is, since it has a false front.

CASINO
HOUSE

WHAT WAS ONCE known as Casino House on Bird Avenue was the main family home of the Emmet family, whose son Robert was involved in the 1798 rebellion and was the instigator of the unsuccessful 1803 rising, for which he was executed. His bedroom in the house had a secret trapdoor that led to an underground passage to a summerhouse, 50 metres away from the main house. This summerhouse was a favourite sanctuary of Robert Emmet's. However, Casino House was only in the possession of his father for four years and was sold in 1801 for £2,000.

THE HOUSE, WITH its many striking internal features, is still in good condition and is currently occupied by the Secretariat of the Secondary Schools of Ireland. Today, the building is known as Emmet House.

MOUNTAINVILLE HOUSE

THIS HOUSE, OPPOSITE Mount Anville convent and school, was
built by Henry Roe, an extremely wealthy nineteenth-century
whiskey distiller. Built on high ground overlooking much of south
County Dublin, a rooftop belvedere was added to take advantage
of those views. The interior of the house was sumptuously
decorated, while the grounds had hothouses, greenhouses,
vineries and peach houses. Later, its name was changed to
Knockrabo, a corruption of the name of Mount Roebuck.
In 1885, the house was bought by Christopher Palles, Lord Chief
Baron of the Court of the Exchequer, and as a very successful
barrister, he had the money to keep the house in impeccable
condition. He even employed two footmen, who wore white ties
and tails, to serve tea in the white and gold drawing room. Palles
died at the house in 1920.

SUBSEQUENTLY, THE MANSION was acquired by the Bank of
Ireland, which had it demolished in 1984 to make room for a
new sports facility for its staff.

OWENSTOWN HOUSE

OWENSTOWN HOUSE, IN Owenstown Park, just off the top of Foster's Avenue, was built around 1800. It is rare among the many big houses that once stood in the Dundrum area; not only has its structure survived intact, but much of the interior has remained virtually unscathed, including fine joinery and plasterwork. During the nineteenth century, it had a variety of owner/occupiers, including Nathaniel Creed, who had a livery lacemaking business close to Dublin Castle, and James Turbett, a wine merchant. The house extends over two storeys and a basement and has the characteristically wide front door typical of the time of its construction.

AT THE TIME of writing, the ground and first floors remain empty and commercial tenants are being sought; the last tenant in this space, a cosmetic clinic, vacated the premises in 2008. The basement area is occupied by an architectural practice.

CROSSROADS
AT DUNDRUM

DUNDRUM ONCE HAD two crossroads, one at each end of the Main Street, but with the development of the Luas bridge, the northern crossroads has long since been swept away.

THE SOUTHERN CROSSROADS in Dundrum have stayed more or less the same. The southern crossroads has still got Campbell's Corner on one corner, the oldest remaining traditional shop in Dundrum. On the opposite corner to Campbell's is Devenney's off-licence, another Dundrum stalwart. That building goes back to 1881 and in earlier years had a variety of uses, including as a short-lived bank branch and as another off-licence. Directly across from Devenney's is the Eagle pub, which goes back to the early twentieth century. The fourth corner at the crossroads, where Main Street turns into Upper

Kilmacud Road, is the only one to have seen major change. For many years, it housed the Leverett & Frye grocery shop, but these days, among its occupiers is Ladbroke's, the bookies.

JOE DALY AND HIS CYCLE SHOPS

JOE DALY SET up his cycle shop in Dundrum in 1951. Daly became a legend in the cycling world, well beyond the confines of Dundrum. It's no surprise that one of the best-known Irish sports people, cyclist Stephen Roche, comes from Dundrum. He was famous for winning the Tour de France in 1987. He no longer races, except for charity, but owns a hotel at Antibes in Provence in southern France as well as a holiday camp for cyclists in Mallorca in Spain. His cycling baton has passed to his son, Nicholas. A commemorative monument to Stephen Roche was erected on the Main Street in Dundrum, but is now beside the pond in the Dundrum Town Centre.

DALY'S SHOP MOVED a couple of times as Dundrum expanded. At one stage, it was on the Main Street, but for nearly ten years now, the shop has been based in a modernistic circular building beside the Luas bridge, almost on the same site where the business started. Today, the shop is run by one of Joe's sons, David Tansey, and it caters for all grades of cyclists, including commuters and dedicated racing cyclists.

A ROYAL VISIT

THIS PHOTOGRAPH SHOWS King Edward VII and Queen Alexandra passing through Dundrum, with what is now the Dundrum Town Centre on the right-hand side of the photograph. They were returning from a visit to Leopardstown racecourse on 29 April 1904.

King Edward VII and his wife visited Dundrum twice during their reign. The second time was 1907 when they attended the opening of the great international exhibition in what is now Herbert Park in Ballsbridge. This was followed by a visit to the races at

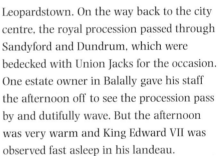

Leopardstown. On the way back to the city centre, the royal procession passed through Sandyford and Dundrum, which were bedecked with Union Jacks for the occasion. One estate owner in Balally gave his staff the afternoon off to see the procession pass by and dutifully wave. But the afternoon was very warm and King Edward VII was observed fast asleep in his landeau.

Another royal visit followed, in 1912, when King George V and Queen Mary travelled through Rosemount and Main Street of Dundrum on their way to visit the Hodgins family who lived at Beaufort, opposite Loreto abbey in Rathfarnham. On this occasion too, the flags were out on Main Street, Dundrum. Four years later, the Easter Rising was staged in central Dublin and the face of Irish politics changed forever. (Image courtesy Michael Fisher)

A BRITISH MONARCH didn't return to this part of Ireland until 2011, when Queen Elizabeth II made a very successful visit.

OLD POST OFFICE

DUNDRUM HAS ONE of the longest established post offices in the Dublin area, outside the city centre. The first post office in Dundrum had opened in 1810, on Main Street (seen here on the left of the photograph), close to where Ryan's pub is now located. Over the years, the post office has had various locations in the centre of Dublin and is currently next door to Campbell's Corner.

Back in the early 1840s, Dundrum residents were getting six postal deliveries a day, compared with five a week now, and these multiple daily deliveries continued for many years. Only within the past twenty years have afternoon deliveries and weekend postal collections been phased out.

THROUGH THE 1840s, Dundrum's postmaster was William Mann. He was a busy
man indeed, since besides running the post office, he was also a land and house agent.
He continued as postmaster until 1865, when his wife became postmistress. For many
years, while the old Harcourt Street railway line was in use, letters for Dundrum arrived
on the train and were then wheeled up Main Street in a handcart for sorting at the post
office, where deliveries were arranged. This arrangement lasted until the early 1950s
when a new sorting office opened at nearby Churchtown.

SAUNDERS HARDWARE SHOP

SAUNDERS HARDWARE SHOP was an old-fashioned emporium that stood on
Main Street, Dundrum, for over fifty years, where Mulveys pharmacy is now located.
Saunders had another shop, which sold drapery and boots and shoes. The hardware shop
had an incredible array of household and garden items, even beds and bedding; it was

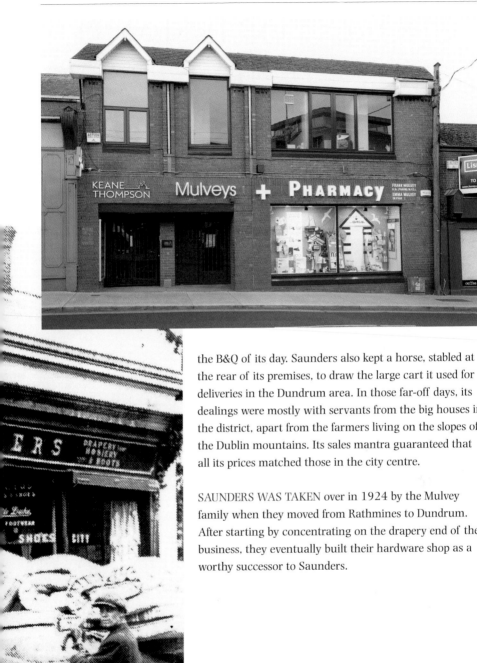

the B&Q of its day. Saunders also kept a horse, stabled at the rear of its premises, to draw the large cart it used for deliveries in the Dundrum area. In those far-off days, its dealings were mostly with servants from the big houses in the district, apart from the farmers living on the slopes of the Dublin mountains. Its sales mantra guaranteed that all its prices matched those in the city centre.

SAUNDERS WAS TAKEN over in 1924 by the Mulvey family when they moved from Rathmines to Dundrum. After starting by concentrating on the drapery end of the business, they eventually built their hardware shop as a worthy successor to Saunders.

CHURCH OF IRELAND, TANEY

THE PRESENT CHURCH was built in 1818, replacing an earlier church. At the same time, several cottages were built beside the church and they too still stand. Initially Taney was very much under the control of St Patrick's Cathedral, which appointed its curates; only in 1851 did the parish gain autonomy. During the 1860s, Dundrum saw a big influx of new residents, drawn by the pure air and the easy access from Dublin with the

new railway line. To cope with the rapid expansion of parishioners, a major renovation of the church got under way, and it was rededicated in 1872. The man who paid for all this work was a wealthy Dublin whiskey distiller, Henry Roe, who at one stage had lived at nearby Mount Anville House. The church interior is still noted for its stained-glass windows and memorials.

TODAY, THE PARISH is the largest and most vigorous Church of Ireland parish in the greater Dublin area. Facilities include the multipurpose parish centre, opened in 1991.

Other older places of worship in the area include the Quaker meeting house on Lower Churchtown Road, dating from 1861. More modern churches include the Church of the Ascension of the Lord in Balally, opened in 1982, and the Church of St John the Evangelist in Ballinteer, which had opened nearly a decade previously, in 1973.

HOLY CROSS CHURCH

IN THE EIGHTEENTH century and well into the nineteenth century, Dundrum didn't exist as a separate parish; it was part of Booterstown. Dundrum parish wasn't created until 1879, two years after the present church was built. Work on the first Catholic chapel in Dundrum, just off the Main Street, had begun in 1813 and was completed in 1830. The first curate, a Fr Powell, was appointed in 1833.

TODAY'S CHURCH IS noted for its striking sandstone façade, mirrored in the adjacent presbytery. The church was substantially extended in 1953, when its length was doubled.

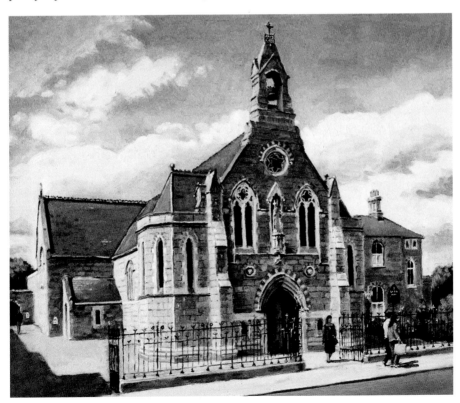

UNCLE TOM'S CABIN

UNCLE TOM'S CABIN on the Dundrum Road at Rosemount goes back to 1842, when it began as a grocery shop with a small bar. In the late nineteenth century, it became a popular stopping off place for cyclists out on excursions; cycling was then a brand new and very popular sport. The pub was bought by James Collins in 1888, grandfather of the

present owner, Tony Collins, meaning the pub has been in the Collins family for close on 130 years. James Collins, already an established vintner, had gone to an auction of pubs, but he had arrived too late to buy the Horse Show House in Ballsbridge, the original intention of his purchase, so he bought the pub in Dundrum instead.

One day, just after the purchase, his wife looked at the book he was reading, *Uncle Tom's Cabin*, and so the pub got the name by which it has been known ever since.

TODAY, THE PUB is noted for its food and also its musical sessions. The old photograph here was taken in 1934; the entrance to the grocery shop is on the left-hand side, while the entrance to the pub is to the right of the picture. In the new photograph, the present owner, Tony Collins, is seen in front of the pub.

ODEON CINEMA

THE ODEON CINEMA at Rosemount, Dundrum, was opened on 1 August 1942.
The exterior of the concrete block building was covered in rustic bricks, while the interior
had an orange, red and gold colour scheme. It was designed by Henry John Lyons and
built by R.G. Kirkham, a Ballsbridge-based builder. The single-screen cinema could seat
750 people and it had parking outside for 500 bicycles in an underground park beneath
the cinema. When it opened, it also had a shop beside the front entrance, while the other
window at the front was used for publicity displays on forthcoming films.

Another interesting aspect of the cinema's interior were the two panels, one on each side of the stage, which lit up in blue and pink at the beginning and end of performances. Apart from the film screenings, live variety shows were often staged. The cinema closed on 31 May 1959, and was sold the following year to the Apollo group. It reopened as the Apollo on 21 April 1961 and managed to last until 26 February 1967, when it closed for good.

SINCE THE 1970S, the building has been owned by the Murphy family and is still known as the Apollo Building. Retail and office units occupy the auditorium. The Murphys opened a wine shop and bar there in 2012, while in 2013, The Work Horse opened, a multi-disciplinary creative centre, including artists' studios and areas for photographers while it has also been used for pop-up dining.

Movies@Dundrum, in the Dundrum Town Centre, opened on 30 September 2005. Large murals with cinematic motifs recall the golden age of the cinema, together with posters and fittings and Art Deco lighting in the twelve auditoria.

MILLTOWN GOLF CLUB

THIS PHOTOGRAPH SHOWS the clubhouse at this renowned south Dublin golf course as it looked on opening day, 28 September 1907. The first captain was a dentist called Fred Davies, regarded as the most influential person in the founding and development of

the club. The first president was William Martin Murphy, who lived at nearby Dartry. He owned the *Irish Independent* and *Evening Herald* newspapers, Clerys department store and the Dublin tramway system, among other interests, and he gained notoriety as the leading employer in the Dublin Lockout of 1913. In 1960, the new clubhouse opened, having been built at a cost of £60,000, or thirty times the cost of the original structure. It replaced the old wooden clubhouse, which had been destroyed in a fire in September 1958. The fire also consumed many old records and resident staff lost all their possessions.

TODAY, THE CLUB continues to develop and thrive, the only golf club and course in the greater Dundrum area.

DUNDRUM BOWL

AFTER THE PYE factory closed in 1987, the northern part of the premises was used for Dundrum Bowl, which began as a rollerblading site. The southern part of the old factory became an H. Williams supermarket. The bowling building was also used for Quasar laser games, which are still played at around nine locations in Ireland. But the centre developed as a bowling arena, with its array of bowling lanes, and for a few years it became a popular leisure location in Dundrum. Another facility located here was an adventure centre for kids called Wally Rabbit's. The building flooded when the levels of the nearby River Slang rose dramatically in 1993 and remained derelict, part of the Pye lands, which became the subject of a famous and protracted tribunal, until construction of the Dundrum Town Centre began soon after the millennium.

The photograph here shows a rear view of the old Dundrum Bowl, with the Holy Rosary church in the distance.

THE OLD DUNDRUM Bowl once stood approximately where the great Mill Pond in the Dundrum Town Centre now stands. Construction of the Town Centre began in 2001 and took four years. The first part of the new centre opened in March 2005. Other features of the Dundrum Town Centre came slightly later, including the cineplex, Movies@Dundrum, and the Mill Theatre. But from the start, the Dundrum Town Centre established itself as an exciting venue for shoppers from far beyond south Dublin. It has over 80,000 sq. metres of floor space and some 170 retail outlets and is now the largest shopping centre in Ireland, attracting around 20 million shoppers a year.

THE GOAT, GOATSTOWN

ONCE THIS PUB was known as Traynor's, and was a thriving establishment in the early years of the twentieth century, when it had a large tree outside, long since chopped down. It was on a main road out of Dublin, at the crossroads in Goatstown but considered a country pub, beyond the reach of city licensing regulations, which ensured a steady trade.

THE PUB WAS bought in 1982 by Charlie Chawke, who has become one of Dublin's best-known and most innovative publicans. In 2003, he survived a robbery, when two raiders intercepted his car just as he was leaving the Goat to lodge the takings. The two robbers were subsequently apprehended and convicted.

OLD POLICE STATION AND COURTHOUSE

THIS PHOTOGRAPH SHOWS Dundrum courthouse and the adjacent police station after it was burned down by the IRA in January 1923. The courthouse had been built in the mid-1850s, followed by the police barracks. After the 1923 fire, both were subsequently rebuilt, while the Garda station was again rebuilt in 1970. A substantial renovation programme is currently under way at the Garda station.

THE COURTHOUSE CLOSED down in the mid-1990s and remained derelict for over a decade. It has since been restored and is now used as part of the Garda station.

ABOUT THE AUTHOR AND PHOTOGRAPHER

HUGH ORAM is a writer and broadcaster who has lived in south Dublin for many years. He has contributed to *The Irish Times* for over thirty years and has made many contributions over a similar time span to RTÉ Radio 1. He has written on a wide variety of topics for many other newspapers, magazines, websites and radio stations both here in Ireland and internationally. He also writes a weekly blog about everyday life and travels in France. These blogs were recently published in book form.

With books, he has written for international travel series published by Michelin, Paris; Random House, New York and Berlitz in the US and has produced many Ireland guidebooks for Appletree Press in Belfast. He has written several company histories, including those of Bewley's cafés, Weirs of Grafton Street, the K Club, Calor Gas Ireland and Flahavan's. He has also written many books on the histories of towns and counties throughout Ireland. Among those he has recently published in this genre have been *Old Achill Island*, *Old County Monaghan*, *Ballsbridge Then & Now*, *The Little Book of Ballsbridge* and the *Little Book of Dundrum*.

PHOTOGRAPHER VINCENT CLARKE'S career began in his father's photography practice in Kells, County Meath, followed by four years with Bill Crimmins in Drogheda while studying photography at Dublin Institute of Technology, Kevin Street. He joined RTÉ Lighting in the late 1970s and worked as Lighting Director on many large productions before retiring in 2012. Vincent brings his extensive knowledge and experience to digital photography with particular emphasis on composition and lighting. This is his second project with The History Press Ireland, having recently completed new photographs for *Donnybrook Now & Then*. For further examples of his work, see www.vclarkephoto.com.

Visit our website and discover thousands of other History Press books.

www.thehistorypress.ie